SOMETIMES YOU GOTTA COMPROMISE

A Light-hearted Look at Model Railroading...and Model Railroaders

Dick Hafer

KALMBACH BOOKS

First printing, 1995. Second printing, 1996.
 Published by Kalmbach Publishing Co., 21027 Crossroads Circle, Waukesha, WI 53187. Telephone: (414) 796-8776.

Printed in the United States of America

Publisher's Cataloging in Publication
(Prepared by Quality Books Inc.)

Hafer, Richard.
    Sometimes you gotta compromise : a light-hearted look
at model railroading—and model railroaders / Dick Hafer.
    p. cm.
    ISBN 0-89024-564-9

    Railroads—Models—Caricatures and cartoons. II. Title.

TF197.H34 1995   625.1'9
                                QBI95-20533

DED ICAT ION

This book is dedicated to my daughter, Diane, who from little on up, wanted to help me build my various layouts.

Thru her, this book has become a reality.

dick hafer

"MODEL RAILROADER"? LISTEN . . . I JUST BASHED ALL MY KITS
AND THEY LOOKED BETTER BEFORE I BASHED THEM.

IT WAS THE ONLY ROOM LEFT FOR MY LAYOUT.

5

HAVE YOU SEEN OUR NEW ZZZZ-SCALE PIKE?

YEAH . . . I'VE NEVER SEEN AN N SCALE SEQUOIA IN M.R.!

PASS THE WORD ... BREAKOUT TONIGHT ... MEET AT
THE PLASTICVILLE FIRE HOUSE!

HAROLD'S ACCESS HATCH WAS RATHER POORLY PLANNED.

WOW! A SCALE FOREST FIRE!! HOW'D YOU DO THAT?!!

10

YEAH ... TECHNICALLY, I GUESS YOU'RE RIGHT — BUT WE ARE
A RELATIVELY NEW CLUB.

11

WENDELL DISCOVERS THAT SAVING MONEY BY USING AN OLD FOOD-PROCESSOR MOTOR ON A TURNTABLE ISN'T A REAL SATISFACTORY SOLUTION.

HERE YOU ARE, SON!

NOW YOU'VE GOT IT!!

ONE OF THE GREAT THINGS ABOUT MODEL RAILROADING IS THAT THERE ARE SO MANY ASPECTS FOR VARYING INTERESTS. I MYSELF LOVE THE ELECTRONICS END OF THE HOBBY!

15

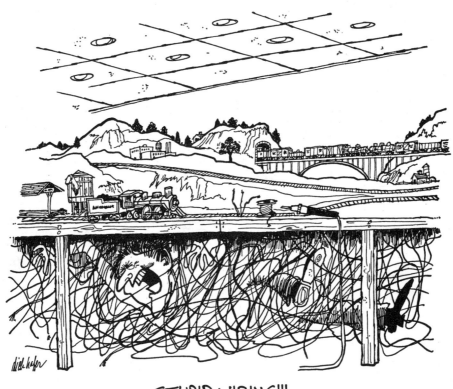

STUPID WIRING!!!

I SAID, "NOT SO FAST!!"

17

SO THE LIGHT SWITCH IS A TEENY BIT INCONVENIENT NOW!
YOU CAN STILL REACH IT!

18

REALLY? YOU'VE BEEN HERE 14 YEARS ALREADY?! YOU DON'T LOOK
A DAY OLDER THAN WHEN YOU ARRIVED!

YEAH, WITH THREE FEET BY SIX INCHES, I WAS PRETTY MUCH LIMITED TO A POINT-TO-POINT LAYOUT.

ALEX WAS DISCOURAGED THAT ALL OF THE REALLY GOOD PROTOTYPE
RAILROADS HAD BEEN MODELED. THEN, HE HAD AN IDEA . . . .

NO SIR, THIS ISN'T PROTOTYPICAL AT ALL! MY BROTHER-IN-LAW WORKS ON A TWO-RAIL PIKE OVER AT PERKIOMAN AVENUE. NOW THERE'S A ROAD!!

WOW! AN AUTHENTIC 3662 MILK CAR IN ITS ORIGINAL BOX
FOR ONLY TWENTY-FIVE BUCKS! WHAT A BUY!!

CONFOUNDED SUPER-GLUE!!

HOW'S THAT FOR SLOW-SPEED OPERATION?!!

YEAH, I'M SCRATCHBUILDING AN N SCALE PET SHOP, AND I'D LIKE A BUNCH OF TEENY AQUARIUMS AND N SCALE TROPICAL FISH.

SHE'S A REAL FUEL-MISER! IT'S BASED ON AN OLD MARX DESIGN.

I'M WRITING YOU A TICKET FOR LOITERING. YOU'VE BEEN STANDING
IN THIS SAME SPOT FOR THREE YEARS!

YOU'RE NOT MARRYIN' ANY GUY WHOSE FATHER'S PIKE
IS AMERICAN FLYER!!

31

NO, HARRY . . . THAT WAS A TILT-UP BRIDGE . . . NOT A LIFT-OUT BRIDGE.

NO . . . A 1% GRADE IS NOT "ONE FOOT VERTICALLY FOR EVERY ONE FOOT HORIZONTALLY."

BOY! AND I THOUGHT G SCALE WAS THE ULTIMATE!

34

I THINK WE'RE ON TO SOMETHING, PROFESSOR SCHILKRAUT!!

WOW!! WHAT A HELIX!

36

YEAH! PERFECT SCALE TREES MADE EASY! POPSICLE STICKS, PING PONG BALLS, AND GROUND FOAM! I'M GONNA SUBMIT IT TO THE "WORKSHOP" COLUMN IN M.R.!

YEP! I GOT A PROMOTION! STARTING TOMORROW I'M GONNA BE
STANDING IN FRONT OF THE PLASTICVILLE AIRPORT!

YESSIR!...SHE'S MY PRIDE AND JOY! AN ACTUAL PIECE OF BALLAST FROM THE MAIN LINE OF THE CHICAGO & NORTH WESTERN, A LITTLE OVER 1/4 MILE OUT OF ELMHURST, ILLINOIS!

NEW! THE H.O. ULTIMATE TRACK CLEANER

41

42

WELL, WELL, MR. MODEL RAILROADERS ANONYMOUS . . . THIS IS A STRANGE PLACE FOR A SIDING!

43

BERNIE . . . THANK GOODNESS YOU'RE THERE! I'VE FINALLY GOT THIS TWELVE-STEP PROGRAM
UNDER CONTROL . . . I THINK. I'M DOWN TO ELEVEN ENGINES AND A CABOOSE!

BACK-SEAT ENGINEER

YEAH ... I READ AN ARTICLE ABOUT USING CARPET FIBERS FOR
GROUND COVER ... BUT IT LOOKED BETTER IN THE M.R. PHOTOS.

IT'S MY NEW SUBWAY LAYOUT.

IT'S THE ONLY WAY WE CAN GET HIM TO SLEEP.

GET OUT'A THERE, SPOT!!

INTO TRAINS, EH?

52

I'LL BE BACK IN 30 MINUTES.

53

FANTASTIC! SCALE FOG!!

OH GOODY! JUST WHAT I LONGED FOR ... A BEAUTIFUL NEW
BRASS ENGINE FOR OUR ANNIVERSARY!

SORRY, MR. KEPLER ... YOUR "MODEL RAILROADER"
DIDN'T COME TODAY. MAYBE TOMORROW.

THANK YOU, MISS "BIRDSEED IS CHEAPER THAN GRAVEL"!
GREAT IDEA!!

MODEL RAILROAD MUSEUM

NEATO!! LOOK AT THIS COOL BUG, EDDIE!

ALL RIGHT!! WHO CARES ABOUT THE MILLION BUCKS?!! I GOT HIS TRAINS!!

NONE OF THE MAGAZINE ARTICLES ABOUT GARDEN RAILROADS
EVER MENTIONED MOLES!

I THINK YOU'VE GOT THE PRESSURE SET JUST A TAD HIGH.

63

YES . . . MY PIKE DEPICTS THE BOSTON & MAINE RR . . . JUNE 14, 1948. . . . 1:35 P.M. . . . THE WESTERN SIDE OF PORTLAND, WITH A SLIGHT OVERCAST. YOU MODEL THE "MID-50'S"?!! IS THAT TINPLATE?

RUDY DISPLAYS HIS PRIDE AND JOY . . . THE WORLD'S FIRST
G SCALE COFFEE-TABLE LAYOUT.

...AND A B&O PA1 ... AND A SIX-STALL ROUNDHOUSE ... AND A READING CONSOLIDATION, WITH SMOKE ... AND ....

A LIKELY STORY!! WHAT DO YOU TAKE ME FOR?!! I DIDN'T COME OUT OF
THE WALTHERS CATALOG YESTERDAY!!

NOT AUTHENTIC?!! IT'S AN ORIGINAL EARLY 1950
PLASTICVILLE VIDEO RENTAL SHOP!!

YEAH ... PASTOR NIETING'S A MODEL RAILROAD BUFF.

WOW! YOU GOT STREAMLINERS TO WORK ON AN EIGHT-INCH RADIUS!!

A GP35! FOR THE FLU?!! WOW!! CAN I GET A GG1 IN CASE OF APPENDICITIS?!

WOW! AN H.O. TOXIC WASTE DUMP!!

O.K., HARRY. THE TUNNEL'S CLEAR. SEND HER ON OVER!

WELL . . . WITH A CLUB, YOU GOTTA BE SENSITIVE
TO ALL OF THE MEMBERS' INTERESTS.

75

. . . ALL THE OTHER GUYS HAVE BRASS PACIFIC LOCOS . . . BUT OH, NO! WE HAVE TO
GET THE STOVE FIXED! . . . SURE . . . THAT'S REAL IMPORTANT!!

SOB! BOB'S GONE!! HE BROKE HIS BASE . . . AND ALL THE SUPER GLUE IN THE WORLD COULDN'T SAVE HIM!!

AHH ... PERHAPS A LITTLE LESS WATER IN THE PLASTER, MARTY.

NO, LETS PICK SOMEPLACE BETTER TO EAT. THEIR FOOD
IS SO . . . "PLASTIC."

HOW ABOUT THAT DIESEL GROWL?!!